Make Your Own Dolls

W9-DEC-478

Ilse Ströbl-Wohlschläger

Make Your Own Dolls

Watson-Guptill Publications

New York

© Otto Maier Verlag, Ravensburg MCMLXVI

Published MCMLXVIII by Watson-Guptill Publications, New York, New York
Library of Congress Catalog Card Number 68 13572
Made and printed in the Netherlands
by The Ysel Press, Deventer

Contents

It began one long winter evening. I was looking for something to do. Paper and pencil were lying near, so I began scribbling. Figures appeared, first lightly suggested but soon taking on more distinct shapes. I drew some Jumping Jacks. Jumping Jacks—the idea led me on, fascinated me and ended by obsessing me. I bought some plywood, fetched the fretsaw, and before I knew it I was at work.

Soon the first—my first—Jumping Jack was flaunting his gay colours and the family was pulling the string approvingly. More Jumping Jacks followed, and some found favour as presents to friends. Of course one can't go on making Jumping Jacks for ever, but the creative urge had seized me and I looked round for other things to do.

A deep rummage in the rag-bag brought forgotten treasures to light in the way of scraps, and I soon came to a decision. I would make cuddly dolls and animals, or whatever you like to call these creatures of cloth and wadding.

My son, almost six, was entranced. He deserted his cars, excavators and railways, to seize on my creations. Hoarded in a wickerwork basket, they went everywhere with him, and at night, of course, one or other of them was allowed to sleep in his bed.

One must have seen for oneself the love and tenderness these simple home-made dolls and toys release in the heart of a child, for a hobby to become a duty. No need to produce masterpieces; we all know that the more imperfect, the better loved they will be.

Of course, as one gradually gains experience, one will want to venture on more difficult things. The dolls will improve in appearance, and the use of a variety of materials will suggest new ideas.

I hope this little book may tempt you to give rein to your imagination and arouse your enthusiasm for a delightful occupation.

The Eskimo Girl on the opposite page is a particularly attractive example of our cuddly dolls

6

Cuddly Dolls and Animals

As usual, it is best to begin with the simplest models. The dolls and animals pictured and described in this chapter are ideal toys for very small children, for they are made, like cushions, of fabric sewn together and filled with soft materials. But even in a childless house they have an attractive use. Their simple shape, in harmoniously combined colours and patterns of fabric, give them a highly decorative effect. Treated as cushions, they lend an original note to the living-room.

The basic procedure is always the same. First draw the outline of your figure on a thin piece of cardboard and cut it out. This gives you a templet to be laid on one side of a folded piece of cloth and drawn round with a pencil or a piece of coloured chalk. The two layers of material are then sewn together accurately along this outline, leaving an opening on the straightest part for turning it inside out and stuffing it. The figure is then cut out about half an inch beyond the seam, afterwards slash-

The pattern is transferred to the folded material by means of a cardboard templet, which can be used again and again

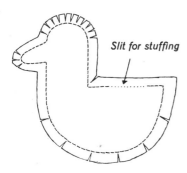

Slit for stuffing

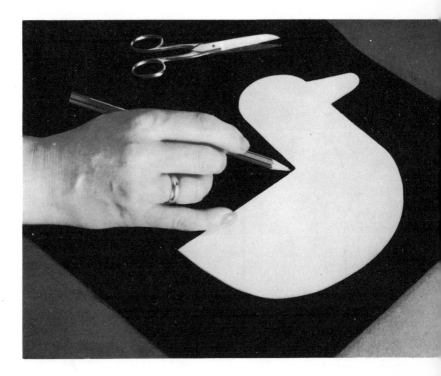

ing this to near the stitching on all curves. Turn inside out, stuff evenly with wadding or absorbent cotton, and sew up the opening. Faces, eyes, hands, beaks, etc., are cut out of felt and sewn on with buttonhole stitch. Hair is made of wool, and braid, lace, ribbons and bows will contribute to an effective finish.

In the patterns shown on pp. 10, 12, 14 and 19, the squares may measure up to ¾ inch

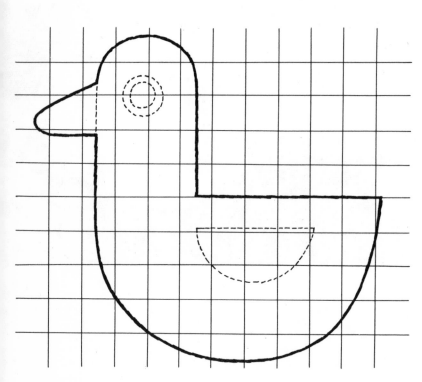

Duck

The duck is a thoroughly unpretentious animal; it can be made from a piece of cloth measuring 8 × 20 inches, and it relies for effect chiefly on colour and pattern. The basic form is very simple and should not present any difficulty even to a beginner. The bill is covered with a piece of coloured felt, and the eyes are made of larger and smaller rounds of felt. The wings are also cut out of coloured felt and sewn on, and the duckling is given a final touch of smartness by a piece of braid trimming round the neck.

A gay newspaper duck

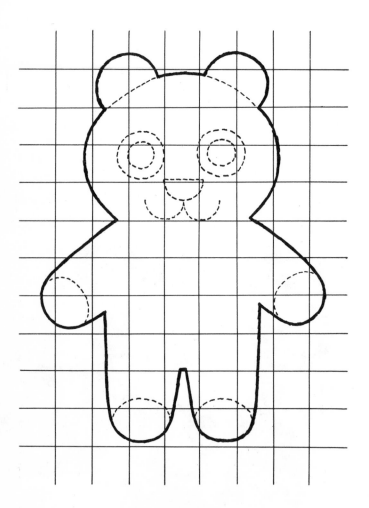

Cloth Bear

The bear will look jolliest made of cloth with a small pattern on it. A scrap of felt can be used to smarten his ears and paws. His eyes are made of two different sized rounds of felt—black on white—and his nose is of black felt and embroidery thread. A necktie gives him a final touch.

Pony

Our pony is tailored in red-and-white check material. Eyes, halter and saddle-cloth are made of felt of different colours. The saddle, especially, lends itself to a gay colour scheme. Black wool is used for the bushy mane and the tail—cut in 4-inch lengths and sewn on to narrow black tape for the mane, and made into a small tassel for the tail. Mane and tail are sewn on to the body after stuffing it, and the pony is finished.

Below: This is how the lengths of wool are sewn on to the tape to represent hair

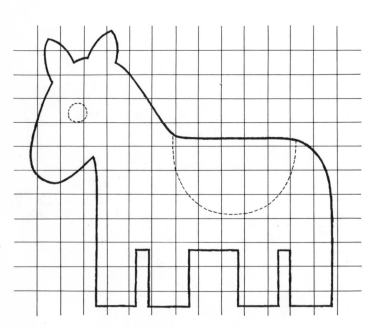

14

Gretel

Gretel ranks as a real little doll, though like all the figures shown so far she has a very simple outline. This not only renders her easier to make, but gives her her special charm. Actually, all the dolls illustrated have the same basic shape. As can be seen in the drawing on p. 19, the most varied figures can be produced by means of slight alterations. To make Gretel we need a piece of check-patterned cloth 12 × 20 inches in size, flesh-coloured felt for the face and hands, various self-coloured scraps of felt and linen, a bit of white lace, and wool for the hair. Collar, stock-ings and apron are made of linen. The white lace is sewn round the apron. Eyes, cheeks, mouth, buttons and shoes are made of felt, and these cut-out shapes are sewn on to the stuffed figure with buttonhole stitching. The hair can be made of red wool, cut in lengths of about 16 inches and sewn on a strip of ribbon or tape of the same colour. The tape is then sewn to the doll's head, and the hair first tied on each side with wool and then formed into two plaits (or braids), both plaits being tied with white ribbon. Last of all, the little nose is stitched on the face in embroidery thread.

Sailor and Clown

A slight alteration in the outline of our doll will easily turn it into a clown or a sailor. Both of these can be made very bright and amusing by a suitable choice of material. What chiefly distinguishes them is their hair. Black yarn is knotted in loops on a bit of canvas to make them a fine mop, and the sailor is given a red pompom on his white hat.

Left: Layers of yarn are looped into canvas (curtain net will do). Facing page: The cutting-out diagram shows how the basic form of the doll can be varied without much practice in drawing

Eskimo Girl

Our Eskimo Girl is outstandingly decorative (see p. 7), although we have kept to a few colours only. The entire body is made of red material measuring 14 × 10 inches. Shoes and head are made of black felt, with a flesh-coloured face, orange cheeks and black eyes. Mouth and nose are embroidered. The hair is made of black yarn knotted on canvas. The only trimming on the frock consists of some decorative braid. But the special effect is produced by the piece of white fur surrounding the face and bordering the hem of the frock. The fur must be cut to shape with great care, with a razor blade, on the wrong side, and then sewn on to the doll with a leather needle.

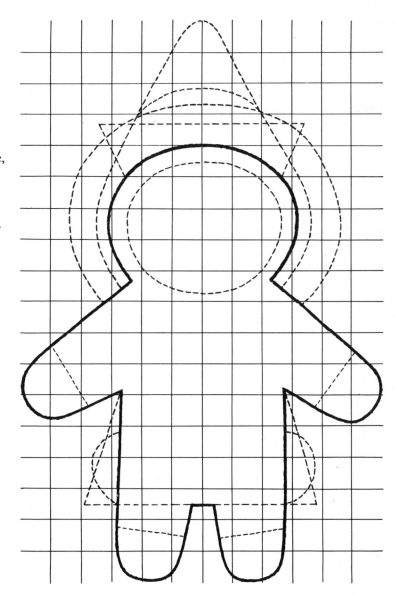

Knitted Dolls

See picture on p. 2

As we sit in the evening, chatting and knitting, knitted dolls take shape almost of their own accord. They cost very little, and give both us and our children a lot of fun.

For our doll we need about one-and-a-half ounces each of red and blue yarn; some flesh-coloured yarn for the face and hands, and black for the hair; a set of four No. 11 needles pointed at both ends; absorbent cotton, or other soft material for stuffing; and some small black buttons.

The body of the doll, with neck, cap and head, is knitted in one piece. The arms and legs are knit separately. We start from the bottom of the torso and work upwards, casting 56 stitches in red yarn on four needles (14 stitches per needle). Knit 30 rows in rounds, then divide your work between two needles (28 stitches per needle) to allow for the armholes. Knit front and back separately for 18 rows.

To make the shoulders, decrease 7 stitches at the beginning of each needle for the next two rows so that only 28 stitches are left for the neck (14 stitches per needle). Now divide 28 stitches among four needles (7 stitches per needle), and knit 8 more rounds. Change to flesh-coloured yarn. Increase 14 stitches for the head by knitting twice every second stitch. At the end of the round, we shall have 42 stitches on four needles.

Now knit 26 rounds plain. Change

the colour of your yarn once
again and knit 26 rounds for the
cap (6 rows red, 6 rows blue, 6 rows
red, and 8 rows blue).
After the 26th row, knit two stitches
together on each needle until only
10 stitches remain (a total decrease
of 32 stitches). Slip the stitches on
to a threaded wool or darning
needle, draw them up, and sew
them together.
Now knit the legs in blue yarn,
picking up 28 stitches for each,
and knit 45 rows plain. Then knit 2
together till only 7 stitches are left
on each needle. Slip these on to a
wool needle, draw them up and
sew them together on the inside.
For the arms, pick up 28 stitches
with red yarn, and knit 30 rows

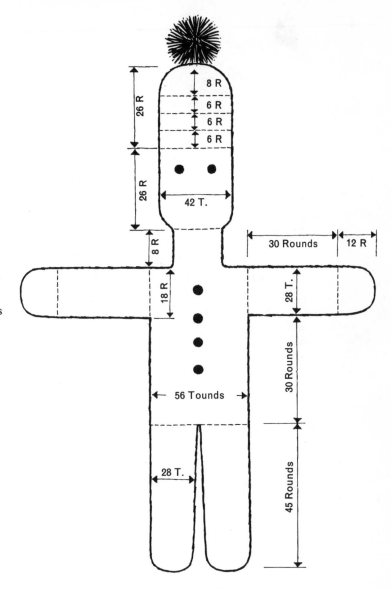

8 R

6 R

6 R

6 R

26 R

26 R

42 T.

8 R

18 R

30 Rounds

12 R

28 T.

30 Rounds

56 Tounds

28 T.

45 Rounds

plain from the armholes, change to flesh-coloured yarn and knit 12 rows for the hands. Then finish off as for the legs.

Knit the muffler in rounds, casting on 28 stitches in blue yarn and knitting about 150 rows plain. Sew up the ends and tie fringes on them. Before stuffing the figure turn it inside out and sew in all the ends of wool to the inside. Then stuff through the open shoulders and sew these up. Fasten a red pompom to the cap, make the hair of black yarn, and finish off the edges of cap and pullover with a cord made of twisted red yarn. Put two buttons on the face for eyes, and four down the front of the pullover. Then wrap the muffler round the neck.

The little black boy is another of the many variants we can make of our knitted dolls

Simple Jointed Doll

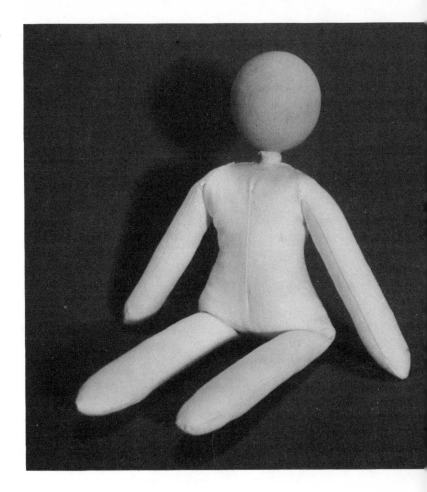

A wooden ball 2 inches in diameter, bored through the middle, a rounded stick to fit the opening, stout white washable material and wadding or absorbent cotton are all the materials needed to make a serviceable doll that will stand up to dressing and undressing by the most assiduous of dolly-mothers.

Finished appearance of the doll

A   Body pattern
B   Leg pattern
C   Arm pattern

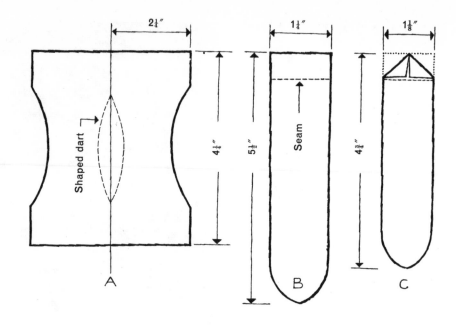

To give our doll a good figure, the pattern of the body is designed with a waist. First transfer the pattern to the folded material, remembering to mark the shaped dart on back and front. Sew the two sides together and stitch the shaped darts. Turn right side out. Leave the shoulder seam open as far as the middle to allow the body to be stuffed and the stick holding the head to be pushed in. Before beginning to stuff the doll, prepare the 'spine'. Glue the wooden ball to the stick, and wind a narrow strip of adhesive tape round the stick at the neck and at the lower end. Now stuff the figure. Stuff one side first, then push in the spine and sew it firmly to the exact centre of the body, then stuff the other side. Sew tubular pieces for the legs and arms, turn and stuff them. Stitch the legs across the top and sew them firmly to the body so that they can move freely backwards and forwards. Stitch the arms across as shown in fig. C, and sew the resulting triangle firmly to the shoulder. The arms can then be moved sideways up and down. Give the doll a handsome wig made of yarn or scraps of fur; make the nose of a little wooden bead, glued or nailed to the face, then paint the eyes and mouth in poster colours.

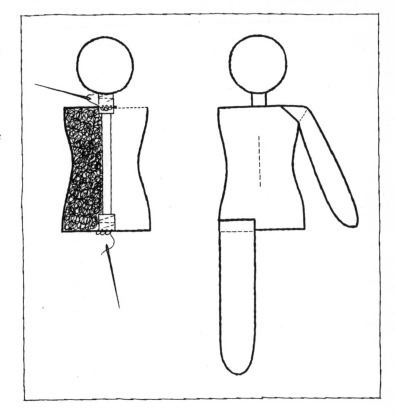

Now we can start making the clothes. Little bright scraps from the rag-bag will be enough to make a regular wardrobe. The basic patterns below show what to do and how to do it.

A   Frock
B   Trousers
C   Costume
D   Pointed cap

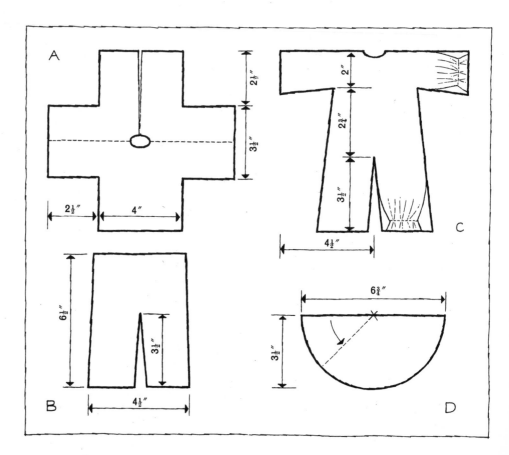

Lisa and Mary

Lisa is a doll beloved of many generations of dolly-mothers (p. 27). Here we have given her thick fair braids, and dressed her in a red frock and a blue apron, with black socks on her feet.

But Mary is a thorough-going teenager. Her modern hair-do in black yarn is in keeping with her blue pullover and red-and-white check trousers.

Dwarf

He could have come straight out of Snow-White's kingdom. His gay suit is tailored in felt, and a thick woollen beard surrounds his merry face.

Clown

Our clown has a costume of white-and-yellow check, with a pointed cap of the same material. As a clown is allowed to be all sorts of colours this one's hair is made of blue yarn. His get-up is finished with a bright red tie and a dark red pompom, and his cap with a purple pompom.

Red Indian Girl

has long black pigtails. Her suit is made of buff-coloured velvet, with fringes at the neck and on the trouser-legs. Jacket and hair are bound round with blue-and-black braid, and a real feather completes the headdress. The Redskin Belle has a necklace of wooden beads.

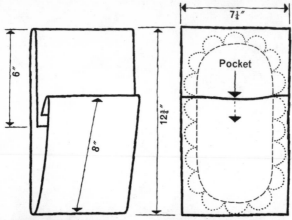

Baby Doll

The baby has rather shorter arms and legs than other jointed dolls. This one has a suit in bright blue or pink check. The cap is made of a bit of lace edging. The pillow is made of lightly starched white muslin, folded as shown in the above diagram and stitched together to shape. The surrounding scallops are then marked and cut out. The pillow is trimmed with lace and edging, and pastel-coloured felt is sewn on the scallops with buttonhole stitching to make a frame to the whole.

Roly-Poly People

Every household keeps a store of
wax paper, tinfoil and the like,
wound on cardboard rolls. Empty
rolls should never be thrown in the
dustbin, for the most amusing
figures can be made of them—just
the thing for table decoration at
parties, and even worthy of a place
on the modern bookshelf.

The materials we need for this
are wooden balls, some pieces of
bright-coloured cloth, odd scraps of
braid, an adhesive, paint, and yarn

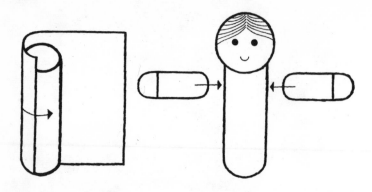

or fur for the hair. The rolls must be cut to a suitable length (about 3½ inches to a diameter of about 1¼ inches), coated with adhesive and covered with a piece of material. The material is cut level with the roll at the bottom, and tucked into the opening at the top. This edge is then smeared with glue, and the wooden ball is set into it. Two simple arms are cut out of cardboard, and have material pasted on them on both sides. Shave the edges neatly and then glue the arms to the body. The lower edge of the rolls can be trimmed with braid. The hair is made of yarn or fur, and eyes and mouth are painted on at the last moment.

Actors for a Puppet Theatre

Hand Puppets

Playing with a puppet theatre is great fun, especially if one can make the puppets oneself. This should be easy for anybody with a little skill, bright fabrics or felt, braid and lace, scraps of wool and fur, and materials for making the head. If ready-made heads, hands and feet are to be found in a hobby shop, so much the better; but if we are to model the heads ourselves, it is best to proceed systematically, and prepare the necessary materials carefully beforehand. Having laid out the materials for several heads in the right order, we can start on 'mass production'. We need pliable cardboard, a roll of adhesive tape, wood wool (or papier mâché mix), paste, muslin, tacking (or basting) thread and plastic modelling material (such as acrylic modelling paste). Work can now begin. First cut out some semicircular pieces of card-

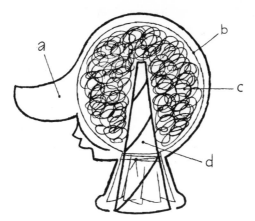

This drawing shows how to model a head.
(a = plastic modelling material
b = muslin, c = wood wool
d = cone made of cardboard)

board, to be rolled over a forefinger into the shape of an ice cream cone, and glued together at the sides. A cone forms the core of a head. Next shape some wood wool (or papier mâché mix) into a ball and stick it over the top of the cone, which has first been coated with adhesive. A square of muslin is then drawn through the (stirred) paste, and pressed over the the ball of wood wool, the ends being bound to the lower end of the cone with thread. This compact object is then dried in a boiler cupboard or an open oven. We now have a solid ball on which to lay a thin coat of plastic and model the face, taking special care to make the nose, cheeks and chin expressive.

Cover the neck with plastic, and form a collar at the bottom of the cone for attaching a garment. The heads can be left to dry overnight. Then we start painting them. For this it is best to use an opaque poster paint, one coat of which will suffice and can afterwards be fixed by a coat of clear varnish. The heads are first given their flesh colour—the ladies a delicate pink, the Clown red-brown and the Robber dark brown. The Witch has a sallow complexion and the Devil a fiery red one. When this groundwork is dry, eyes, cheeks and mouth can be added, after which the transparent varnish is applied. Now come the hair-dos. Yarn is equally suitable for the

Below: The Devil and the
Policeman have magnificent
beards and heads made of
fur. Right: The chief
figure—the Clown

locks of a Princess, Gretel's
pigtails, the unkempt mop of the
Clown and the Witch, but scraps
of fur make the most striking
beards and hair.

The same hair-dos look equally
well on ready-made wooden heads,
but these look best left in their
natural colour, with only eyes,
cheeks and mouth painted on them.
They are also very attractive with
eyes and cheeks cut out of felt
and glued on.

Clothes for all are cut on a single
basic pattern. Felt was used for all
the modelled puppets. Pattern A
shows the cut. Flesh-coloured
hands are sewn into the short
sleeves in such a way that the
player's fingers can be inserted in

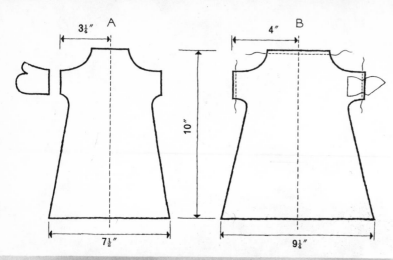

A   3¼″   B   4″   10″   7½″   9¼″

them. Accessories like veils, lace, collars, gold braid, with a crown for the Princess, a pointed cap for the Clown, a slouch hat for the Robber, etc., complete these single garments.

For a wooden-headed puppet, pattern B is designed to give the garment greater fullness, which is particularly useful when grownups are working the puppets. In this case materials of any sort can be used. The finished garment is drawn up round the neck and the wooden hands with small running stitches.

The Clown has trousers sewn to the front of his garment, to take his wooden legs.

Now we're ready. We slip our hands into the dolls. The play can begin.

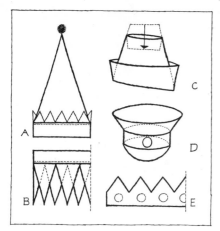

Left: Grandmother and Grand-
father
Right: The Robber with his
slouch hat and his sack
The drawings show the cut of the
clothes and accessories
(A = Clown's cap, B = ruff,
C = Grandfather's hat, D =
Policeman's cap, E = King's
crown)

Top left: the King
Right: boy and girl
Far right: the Queen,
    a wooden doll

44

Puppets on Sticks

for a miniature theatre easily set up on the kitchen table, and as easily taken down again, are amusing and practical, and made at home. All you need is a threefold screen made of cardboard, with an opening at the top, which can be folded flat when not in use, and a flower-pot full of 'stick' puppets, made in the following way.

Materials: pipe cleaners, perforated wooden balls about $\frac{1}{2}$ and $1\frac{1}{4}$ inches in diameter, small round sticks to fit the holes in the balls, wooden beads, coloured felt, scraps of material, lace, ribbon and braid, yarn and fur, adhesive and a little stuffing.

The patterns for the clothes are cut out of cardboard stout enough to stand repeated use, and drawn round on any sort of material. The garment is stitched on the doubled material and then cut out, leaving ample turnings, hemmed, pressed and turned right side out. Finish it with whatever trimming best suits the character.

The framework of the puppet is made out of the balls, pipe-cleaners and stick. The stick should be about

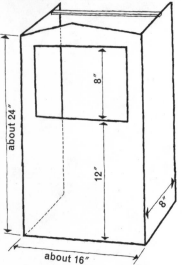

Above: Granny and granddaughter
Left: How to make the theatre

about 24"

8"

12"

8"

about 16"

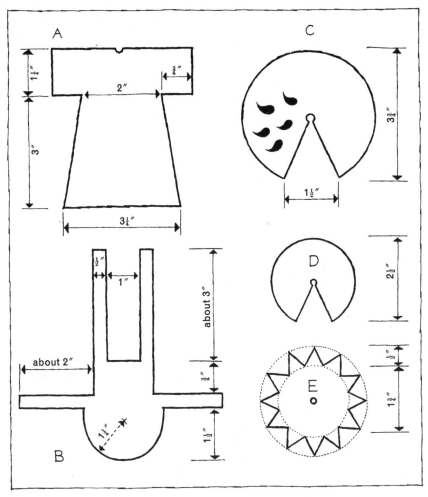

A

1¼″

2″

3″

¾″

3¼″

B

½″

1″

about 3″

about 2″

¾″

1½″

1¼″

C

3¾″

1½″

D

2½″

E

½″

1¾″

Clothes patterns:

A Basic garment patterns
B Granddaughter's apron
C King's collar
D Smaller collar
E Clown's ruff

47

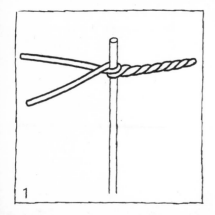
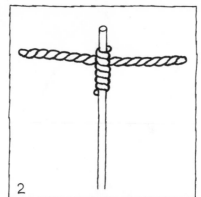
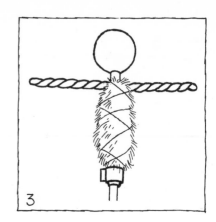

a foot in length and have two pipe-cleaners fixed firmly round it to right and left, near the top, with their ends twisted closely together. A third one is then twisted over the junction of the arms and a little way down the stick, to keep them in place. The body is formed of stuffing wound round the stick, held together with thread, and prevented from slipping by a strip of adhesive tape at the bottom. Slip the garment over the framework and glue the big ball to the top. The smaller balls are glued to the pipe-cleaner arms to form the hands.

Below: Policeman and Robber, Right: the Queen, Far right: the King. Yarn or fur is used for the hair, metal foil and felt for head coverings. Each head is given a wooden bead for a nose, painted eyes and, unless the bottom of the face is covered by a mighty beard, a mouth.

Jumping Jacks

The age of mechanical toys has driven the Jumping Jack out of nearly all our playrooms, and it is all the more delightful to come across him again unexpectedly. Let us bring him to life once more, not only there but as a decorative wall-hanging in the living-room. Of course we must make him ourselves. It's fun to do, and calls for a little technical knowledge, because the mechanism must function properly.

To do the work well, we need a fret-saw outfit, thin plywood, thin brass screws with nuts to fit, strong string, a length of cord, a small perforated wooden ball and some paint. Then we take a pencil and design our Jumping Jack. He consists of seven separate parts —body, two arms, thighs and lower legs.

As may be seen from the diagram, the body is completely symmetrical, so that we need only design one side of it, starting from the axial

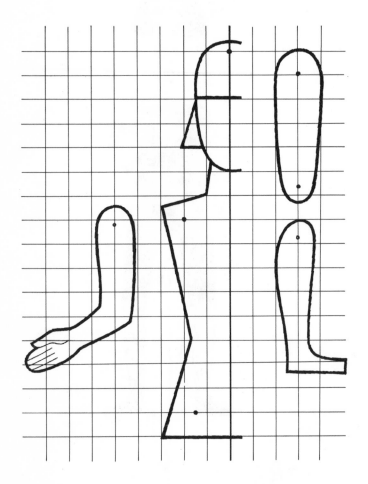

line, and then transfer the shape, mirror fashion, to the other side. Arms and legs are also alike. We now trace all these shapes on the plywood and saw them out, afterwards smoothing all the sawn edges with sandpaper. Then we drill holes at the joints to take the screws and for attaching the pulling mechanism. We also bore a hole through the top of the head for hanging the figure up. Next we start painting it. All the parts must first have an undercoat of white, and then our Jumping Jack can be given a bright-coloured costume, Tempera paints are very suitable for this. All the painted parts must be finally coated with colourless varnish. The varnish must be absolutely dry before the figure is mounted. The members must be accurately assembled and first lightly fastened together with the brass screws, so that the string can be passed through. After this the nuts are screwed on, leaving room for the arms and legs to move easily, and then the protruding end of the screw is nipped off. The insertion of a washer will prevent the moving parts from rubbing over each other wearing off the paint.

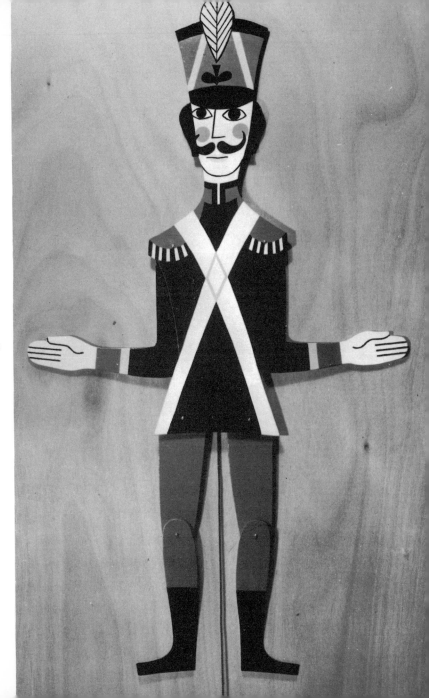

The drawing below shows how the pulling-string is connected. The visible part of the mechanism consists of a piece of cord with a small wooden ball attached to the end of it.

The Jumping Jack is hung up on the wall, and we can start pulling.

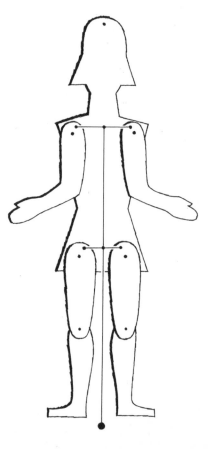